Southeast Asia

Monika Davies

Consultants

Kerry Shannon, Ph.D.
Assistant Professor of History
California State University, Dominguez Hills

Roger B. Han, M.A.
Freelance Educator and Business Consultant

Mab Huang, Ph.D.
Political Science Professor

Brian Allman
Principal
Upshur County Schools, West Virginia

Publishing Credits

Rachelle Cracchiolo, M.S.Ed., *Publisher*
Emily R. Smith, M.A.Ed., *SVP of Content Development*
Véronique Bos, *Vice President of Creative*
Dani Neiley, *Editor*
Fabiola Sepulveda, *Series Graphic Designer*

Image Credits: p.4 Shutterstock/2p2play; p.5 iStock/Grace Thang; p.7 (bottom) Alamy/
Khair Mispan/Stockimo; p.9 (top) Shutterstock/Azmi Pamungkas; p.14 (bottom) iStock/
Cheryl Ramalho; p.15 (bottom) iStock/Heckepics; p.17 (bottom) Shutterstock/Sony
Herdiana; p.19 (top) Shutterstock/Uwe Aranas; p.20 Alamy/Asia File; p.21 Shutterstock/
Shahjehan; p.23 Shutterstock/Lano Lan; p.24 Shutterstock/R. Bociaga; p.25 Shutterstock/
Adirach Toumlamoon; p.27 (top) iStock/Joel Carillet; p.27 (middle) Shutterstock/Azad
Pirayandeh; all other images from iStock and/or Shutterstock

Library of Congress Cataloging-in-Publication Data

Names: Davies, Monika, author.
Title: Southeast Asia / Monika Davies.
Description: Huntington Beach, CA : Teacher Created Materials, Inc, [2023]
| Includes bibliographical references and index. | Audience: Ages 8-18 |
Summary: "Southeast Asia is a region on the rise. Thousands of ethnic
groups call this region home. Hundreds of languages are spoken here.
Some consider Southeast Asia to be the world's most diverse region!
Parts of Southeast Asia have seen great growth in previous decades.
However, this area of the world also faces great civic challenges. Let's
get to know this richly diverse part of the planet"-- Provided by
publisher.
Identifiers: LCCN 2022038437 (print) | LCCN 2022038438 (ebook) | ISBN
9781087695181 (paperback) | ISBN 9781087695341 (ebook)
Subjects: LCSH: Southeast Asia--Juvenile literature.
Classification: LCC DS521 .D38 2023 (print) | LCC DS521 (ebook) | DDC
959--dc23/eng/20220817
LC record available at https://lccn.loc.gov/2022038437
LC ebook record available at https://lccn.loc.gov/2022038438

Shown on the cover is Yen Bai, Vietnam.

This book may not be reproduced or distributed in any
way without prior written consent from the publisher.

TCM | Teacher
Created
Materials

5482 Argosy Avenue
Huntington Beach, CA 92649
www.tcmpub.com
ISBN 978-1-0876-9518-1
© 2023 Teacher Created Materials, Inc.

Table of Contents

Exploring Southeast Asia 4

Travel through Time 6

Geography of Southeast Asia. 12

Economic Growth and Change. 18

Civics and Government Leadership 22

Rapid Changes 26

Map It! 28

Glossary 30

Index 31

Learn More!. 32

rice fields in Mù Cang Chải, Vietnam

Exploring Southeast Asia

Southeast Asia is home to more than half a billion people. Each country there has its own languages and cultures. Hundreds of ethnic groups live throughout the region.

There are two parts to Southeast Asia: the mainland and the **maritime** area. Mainland Southeast Asia consists of six countries. Thailand lies at the heart of this area. Tucked beside it is Cambodia. To the north is the country of Myanmar (also known as Burma). Laos and Vietnam are to the east. Singapore is located farther south. It is a tiny island country.

The maritime area is mostly made up of groups of islands. These countries are called **archipelagos**. This includes Indonesia, Malaysia, and the Philippines. Brunei lies on the island of Borneo, near the Philippines. Timor-Leste (also known as East Timor) is a small island country. It is found in the southernmost part of Southeast Asia.

street market in Singapore

Pacific Ocean

Philippine Sea

MYANMAR
LAOS
THAILAND
CAMBODIA
VIETNAM
Gulf of Thailand
South China Sea
PHILIPPINES
BRUNEI
MALAYSIA
SINGAPORE
INDONESIA
Java Sea
TIMOR-LESTE

Bangkok, Thailand

5

Travel through Time

The history of Southeast Asia spans thousands of years. The region is made up of 11 distinct countries. Each one has its own historical time line. But certain events over the years affected all of them. Let's examine those key events as well as diverse aspects of the region.

First People

Thousands of years ago, people started living in Southeast Asia. Humans may have lived in the area as early as 73,000 years ago. In Thailand, these first people likely grew rice. They used metal tools.

In time, kingdoms were formed in Southeast Asia. Kingdoms are lands ruled by royalty. A royal ruler is usually a king or a queen. One powerful kingdom was the Khmer Empire. Starting in the 800s CE, this kingdom ruled most of Southeast Asia. This included large parts of Cambodia and Thailand. Laos was once part of the empire, too. So was southern Vietnam.

Angkor Wat, Cambodia

The Khmer are remembered for their astounding buildings. They also built roads and canals. Most notably, they built the temples of Angkor Wat. These temples were dedicated to Hindu gods. These temples still stand tall. They are now world-famous attractions. People can visit them in Cambodia.

The Khmer enjoyed celebrating. Fireworks, music, and dancing were key parts of their culture. They also had wrestling matches and horse races.

The "Sea People"

The first people to live in Singapore were the Orang Laut tribe. *Orang Laut* is a Malay term for "sea people." They gathered their food from the ocean, and they fished and lived on boats. Now, the Orang Laut have become part of the Malay ethnic group in Singapore.

Like the Orang Laut, the Sama-Bajau peoples rely on their ocean lifestyles.

Between 849 and 1300, the Kingdom of Pagan existed. Pagan was a walled city. It was located in the modern-day area of central Myanmar. The Irrawaddy River ran alongside the city.

People in the kingdom traveled far and wide. They helped spread the religion of Buddhism. It is thought that thousands of Buddhist temples and pagodas were built in the Kingdom of Pagan. It is hard for historians to know exactly how many were built. They think that part of the ancient city was washed away by the river. Today, there are more than 3,000 temples, pagodas, and other buildings still standing.

These ancient kingdoms did not rule forever. War was constant between kingdoms. But the kingdoms made their marks on history. Each had a lasting cultural impact on the surrounding area.

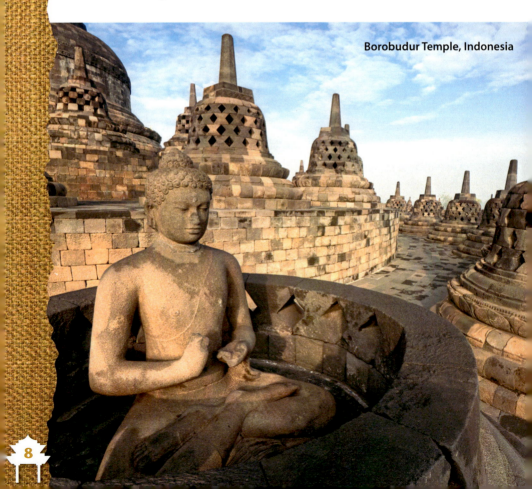

Borobudur Temple, Indonesia

A farmer in Indonesia dries black pepper.

The Fight for Spices

In the past, there was huge demand for spices across the world. Southeast Asia is home to many flavorful spices. Nutmeg was once only found in this region. Black pepper was also a valuable find here. Parts of Southeast Asia became known as the Spice Islands.

Western powers took note of the Spice Islands. They wanted to control access to the region's resources. **Colonizers** invaded the region. This changed Southeast Asia.

Significant Spices

Southeast Asia is still world-famous for growing key spices found in many kitchens. Some significant spices include ginger, cloves, and nutmeg. At one point, eastern Indonesia was the only place where cloves and nutmeg were grown!

nutmeg

Independence

Colonizers affected life in Southeast Asia for hundreds of years. A few European countries and the United States invaded the land. And during World War II, Japan **conquered** colonies in Southeast Asia. But, people in the region wanted to be free from the rule of other countries. It took a few decades. But by 1957, most Southeast Asian countries were independent. Other countries no longer controlled the region. Brunei was the last country to get full independence in 1984.

Languages

There are more than 6,500 languages spoken worldwide. At least 1,000 are spoken throughout Southeast Asia! Each country has a range of languages. But most countries have a main language. In Myanmar, it's Burmese. The Thai language is spoken most in Thailand. Many Cambodians speak Khmer. Malay is heard in Malaysia. Each language spoken in the region is unique.

Living Languages

It is estimated that roughly 150 languages are spoken in the Philippines. But the country does have two official languages. One is Filipino. The other is English. Most people speak one of those two languages.

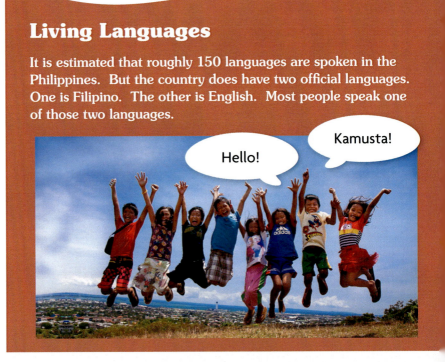

Religions

Most people in the region practice one of three religions. Buddhism is one. It's practiced in most areas of the mainland. About 90 percent of people in Myanmar practice Buddhism. Around 40 percent of the region's people practice Islam. This is because of a large Muslim population in Indonesia. Christianity is also practiced.

Singapore is one of the most religiously diverse countries. At least 10 faiths are practiced there. In contrast, Timor-Leste is one of the least diverse. Nearly 98 percent of its people are Catholic.

mosque in Indonesia

temple in Myanmar

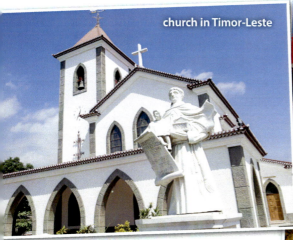
church in Timor-Leste

Geography of Southeast Asia

An easy way to locate the region of Southeast Asia is to pinpoint China and India on a map. Southeast Asia is found south of China and east of India. Much of the region also lies between two oceans. To the west is the Indian Ocean. The Pacific Ocean is found east of the region.

Southeast Asia is often divided into two zones. There is the mainland and the maritime zone. These two areas have many physical features.

Mainland Zone

The mainland is connected to the Asian continent. This area is south of China. The mainland is also closely linked to northwestern India.

Mekong River

Long mountain ranges define the mainland. These ranges mostly stretch from north to south. Sometimes, these mountain ranges serve as country borders. For instance, an **interlinking** mountain range is found to the northwest of the region. These mountains separate India and Myanmar. One part of this range is called the Nāga Hills.

Deep river valleys lie between the mainland's mountainous sections. There are five major river systems that run through the mainland. One large system is the Irrawaddy River. Another is the Salween River. But the Mekong River is perhaps the most well-known. It is Southeast Asia's longest river. It flows through six countries. They are China, Myanmar, Laos, Thailand, Cambodia, and Vietnam.

Tectonic Transformations

The movement of big tectonic plates helped define Southeast Asia's landforms. These plates are large, moving pieces on the earth's crust. As plates moved, the region's lands changed shape. This is partly why Southeast Asia is home to so many long mountain ranges.

the Nāga Hills

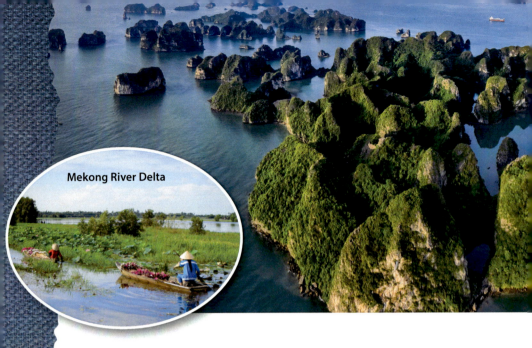

Mekong River Delta

The Mekong River is one of the world's greatest waterways. Millions of tons of rice are grown near the river every year. The river is also a source for freshwater fish. Many people depend on the Mekong.

The Irrawaddy River is a shorter river. It weaves through western Myanmar. But the river's delta spreads wide. A delta is a triangle-shaped area of land. It forms when a river splits into smaller rivers. These smaller rivers then run into a larger body of water. A delta area often has **fertile** soil. Most people in Southeast Asia live near a delta.

Dry, Hot, or Wet?

For most Southeast Asian countries, there are three climate seasons: dry, hot, and wet. Typically, the dry season runs from November to February. Temperatures rise sharply for the "hot season" from March to June. And **monsoon** rains fall in the wet season between June to October.

Heavy monsoon rains can cause flooding.

Hạ Long Bay, Vietnam

Maritime Zone

The maritime zone is made up of islands. This area has thousands of islands. Some islands are sizable, such as Borneo. Others are small dots of land on the water.

Each island looks different. Some are mountainous. But others are fairly flat. Most islands face the same challenges, though. Earthquakes are common in the area. Volcanic activity also occurs. For instance, Indonesia has more than 100 active volcanoes! Climate change is another issue. It causes sea levels to rise, which threatens the islands.

The region's islands rely on the waters that border their lands. **Shallow** waters are found between many islands. This makes it easy to travel by boat to and from places. Trade between countries is often done by boat. In the past, this was also how people sent messages to different islands.

Cai Rang floating market in Vietnam

Rain Forests

Rain forests are rich **ecosystems**. A large variety of species can only be found in these wet places. Almost 15 percent of the world's tropical forests are in Southeast Asia. Some of the largest rain forests are found in Indonesia. Malaysia is also home to large sections of rain forest.

But vast parts of these forests are destroyed every year. Mostly, this is done to make room for oil palms. Oil palms help create palm oil. This cooking oil is in high demand around the world. Rain forests are also threatened by the practice of logging. This is the process of cutting down trees to use for lumber.

Natural Resources

Many **plantations** are found in Southeast Asia. People grow different crops there. In some parts of the region, they grow rubber and bananas. They also grow tea and spices.

Southeast Asian countries are working to produce more exports. These are products sold to other countries. Some countries, such as Indonesia, produce petroleum. In the Philippines, nickel is a top export. Copper and gold are also important exports in this region.

Cultural Geography

Diverse ethnic groups live in Southeast Asia. For example, Cambodia is home to the Khmer peoples. Burmans make up two-thirds of Myanmar's population. Some countries have several ethnic groups. The Philippines is one example. One large group is the Tagalog. The Cebuano, Ilocano, and Bicol groups are also found there.

tropical rain forest in Malaysia

Scarce Species

Southeast Asia is home to many of the world's rarest species. The orangutan is an ape with vivid red fur. It's one of the species that is only found in the wild in Southeast Asia. The Javan rhinoceros and silvery gibbon are two other species that only live in the rain forests of Southeast Asia.

orangutans

Workers harvest tea in Indonesia.

Economic Growth and Change

Southeast Asia plays a major role in the global economy. The region first traded spices grown by farmers. Nowadays, the region's main exports are raw materials.

Agriculture

Most people in Southeast Asia live in rural areas. Nearly 75 percent live outside cities. In this region, farming is how most people make a living.

Wet-rice cultivation is the most common form of farming in the region. **Consistent** water supply is needed for this. Rice is the region's top crop. In areas with less rainfall, crops such as corn and legumes are grown. Cash crops are planted in some places. These are crops planted and grown just to be sold to others. These farmers do not eat or use their own crops. In Malaysia, rubber trees are one example. Cacao, coffee, and spices are also cash crops. These crops are grown on plantations.

workers in a rice field

Timber is loaded onto a truck in Malaysia.

Logging

Commercial logging is also common in the region. Southeast Asia is home to large tropical forests. There is demand for wood products across the world. Teak is one common export. Mahogany is another. These woods are used for building and furniture construction.

A Young Crowd

Many young people call Southeast Asia home. About half of the population is under 30 years old! This young crowd, like other young people around the world, is facing some global issues, including climate change. How do you think young people will direct the region's future?

Industrialization

Southeast Asia is rapidly changing. **Industrialization** is changing life in the region. These changes began a few decades ago. The economies of several countries there are quickly growing.

Manufacturing has made a big difference in the region. Factories are a common sight. Thousands of products are made. Many goods are exported from these countries.

Singapore has a strong economy. In fact, it is one of Asia's strongest. Singapore produces and sells many products. One export is electronics. Malaysia also exports many electronics.

Other countries export goods, too. Vietnam processes a lot of food and beverages. This includes seafood, coffee, and tea. Indonesia exports rubber and palm oil around the world. The Philippines produces goods including clothing, electronic parts, and food and beverages.

Workers assemble electronics at a factory in Singapore.

Leaders of Southeast Asia meet to make decisions.

The Role of ASEAN

This region is coming together to work on their future. ASEAN stands for Association of Southeast Asian Nations. ASEAN is an international group. There are 10 countries in the group. They include almost all countries in Southeast Asia. ASEAN was first built to help with economic growth. The organization aims for cooperation between governments as well. Their goals are future-oriented. Their website notes that they are looking toward peace and freedom for the region.

Digital Spending

In Southeast Asia, 70 million people shopped online for the first time during the COVID-19 pandemic. Experts believe that by 2026 there will be 380 million online shoppers in Southeast Asia. Countries in this region have seen other changes in spending habits, too. It has become more common to pay digitally rather than with cash, a debit card, or a credit card.

Civics and Government Leadership

Every Southeast Asian country has its own government. Each is meant to serve its citizens. But leadership looks different from place to place.

Democracy

A democracy is a system of government. In a democracy, everyone has equal rights. There are free elections. People can speak up about issues. In Southeast Asia, democratic processes were once less common.

In the 1980s, change slowly began. A desire for democracy rose in the region. People pushed for change. They wanted more freedoms.

The Philippines is one example. A **dictator** once held power there. This shifted in the late 1980s. An election was held. The dictator in power lost. The elected leaders took office. They created a new **constitution**. The government shifted from a dictatorship to a democracy.

Corazon Aquino served as the president of the Philippines from 1986 to 1992.

A woman casts a vote in an election in Malaysia.

Authoritarian Power

Authoritarian power is used in some governments. It supports less freedom. One leader or party holds all the power. Freedoms are limited. Elections may not be free or fair. Lately, the Southeast Asian region is seeing a rise in this kind of power. In some countries, armed forces have taken control. The people in power were not elected by citizens.

What Does It Mean to Be Free?

Freedom House is a group that supports worldwide democracy. Every year, they release a report. This report scores how "free" each country is. The report looks at political rights, such as the right to vote or freedom of expression. In Southeast Asia, only Timor-Leste was labeled "free" in 2021.

Timor-Leste

Myanmar is under this kind of authoritarian leadership. From 1962 to 2011, armed forces ruled the country. **Activists** pushed for reform. A new constitution was put in place. For a few years, the country had a democratic government. In 2015, elections were held.

Some people argued this leadership was not fully democratic, though. Then, in 2021, a coup occurred. This is when armed forces take control. These takeovers are often violent. Myanmar then returned to an authoritarian rule.

People in Myanmar protest against the military coup in 2021.

A Citizen Response

The village of Gumuk Indah is on the island of Java in Indonesia. In March 2020, as COVID-19 began to spread, residents gathered to create a plan. They decided to set up their own task force. Their goal was to stop the spread of the virus in their community. The task force promoted handwashing and set up checkpoints run by volunteers. Local tailors even made masks. This citizen-led response helped the community take action during an uncertain time.

What's Next?

Leaders in some Southeast Asian countries rule by force. This includes leaders in Cambodia. Laos is another example. Other countries, such as Thailand, have reduced freedoms over the years.

In the region, some people are unsure about the best way forward. They wonder if democracy helps or **hinders** growth. Others strongly believe in democracy. Starting in 2020, student groups in Thailand led more than 200 protests in the country. They pushed for democratic reforms.

Most Southeast Asian countries are not fully free. But what is best for one country may not be best for another. The region keeps changing and growing.

Leaders play an important role in directing the region's future. But the people of Southeast Asia will help direct their future, too.

People march in Thailand during an anti-government protest.

Rapid Changes

Southeast Asia is a richly diverse corner of the world. Hundreds of ethnic groups call this area home. At least 1,000 different languages are spoken here.

There are 11 countries in this region. Life in each country is distinct. Living in Vietnam is vastly different from living in Singapore. But each country shares parts of history with the others.

The last century brought sizable changes to Southeast Asia. Decolonization began. Democracy rose—but may be declining. Economies are expanding for some countries. Other economies in this region are still struggling.

Life in this diverse region will keep changing. Most people still work as farmers there. But how people make a living in Southeast Asia will likely shift in the coming years. More people are purchasing items they need online. People are moving from rural areas to urban areas. As lifestyles transform, so will the outlook of the region's future.

Southeast Asia is in a state of transition. Its future looks bright as this part of the world continues to grow. It's tough to predict what lies ahead. But one thing remains true: Southeast Asia is a region on the rise.

Climate Change in Southeast Asia

The entire planet is facing issues related to climate change. But some regions are more vulnerable to climate change. This includes Southeast Asia. Experts point out that climate change is causing sea levels to rise. Higher waters lead to floods and typhoons. Southeast Asia is surrounded by water. Climate change is likely to have a huge impact on the region.

people at a market in the Philippines

a farmer in Cambodia

people working in Singapore

Map It!

It's time to collaborate and map out this diverse region of the world. With a group, create a political map.

1. Write a list of all the countries in Southeast Asia. Remember, there are 11 in total!

2. Using a large sheet of paper, sketch outlines of the countries in Southeast Asia. Label each country with its name.

3. Which countries are part of the mainland zone? Which countries are part of the maritime zone? Label each country as "mainland" or "maritime."

4. Look up each country's capital city. Draw a dot to pinpoint each capital on your map. Label each dot with the capital's name.

5. What are the major oceans that border Southeast Asia? Label all nearby oceans.

6. What is one major river that runs through Southeast Asia? Draw and label the river.

Marina Bay Sands hotel in Singapore

Glossary

activists—people who take strong action to make changes in politics or society

archipelagos—groups of islands

colonizers—distant countries that take over areas of land and control them

conquered—took control of something by using force

consistent—always the same; steady

constitution—a document that describes the system of government for a country, state, or organization

dictator—someone who rules a country with complete authority, often in a cruel way

ecosystems—groups of living and nonliving things that make up environments and affect each other

fertile—able to produce many plants or crops

hinders—makes something slow or challenging

industrialization—the process of building and operating numerous factories and businesses in a city or country

interlinking—connecting two or more things together

manufacturing—producing goods or products

maritime—of or relating to the ocean or sea

monsoon—a periodic wind in the Indian Ocean and southern Asia that brings heavy rains in the summer

plantations—large areas where crops are grown

shallow—having a short distance from a surface to the bottom; not deep

ancient temples in Bagan, Myanmar

Index

Angkor Wat, 6–7

Aquino, Corazon, 22

ASEAN, 21

Borneo, 4, 15

Brunei, 4–5, 10

Cambodia, 4–8, 10, 13, 16, 21, 25, 27

China, 12–13

India, 12–13

Indonesia, 4–5, 8–9, 11, 16–17, 20, 24

industrialization, 20

Irrawaddy River, 8, 13–14

Japan, 10

Khmer Empire, 6–7

Laos, 4–6, 13, 25

Malaysia, 4–5, 10, 16, 18–20, 23

Mekong River, 13–14

Myanmar, 4–5, 8, 10–11, 13–14, 16, 24

Orang Laut, 7

Philippines, the, 4–5, 10, 16, 20, 22, 27

rain forests, 16–17

Sama-Bajau, 7

Singapore, 4–5, 7, 11, 20, 26–27

Thailand, 4–6, 10, 13, 25

Timor-Leste, 4–5, 11, 23

Vietnam, 4–6, 13–15, 20, 26

World War II, 10

Learn More!

For two decades, a dictator was the head of state in the Philippines. The people pushed for democracy in the 1980s. One of the leaders of this movement was Corazon Aquino. She was later elected president of the Philippines. Research Aquino's life, and answer the following questions:

- What is her story?
- How did she come to be the first female president of the Philippines?
- What conflicts did she solve?
- Create a presentation to show her political achievements. Try to find quotations or pictures for your presentation.

Manila, Philippines